IT STARTED *with a* HELMET

*A Retired Firefighter's Return
to New York City the Day Before 9/11*

Gerald Sanford *and*
Chris Griffith

IT STARTED WITH A HELMET
A RETIRED FIREFIGHTER'S RETURN TO NEW YORK CITY THE DAY BEFORE 9/11

iUniverse books may be ordered through booksellers or by contacting:

iUniverse
1663 Liberty Drive
Bloomington, IN 47403
www.iuniverse.com
844-349-9409

Because of the dynamic nature of the Internet, any web addresses or links contained in this book may have changed since publication and may no longer be valid. The views expressed in this work are solely those of the author and do not necessarily reflect the views of the publisher, and the publisher hereby disclaims any responsibility for them.

Any people depicted in stock imagery provided by Getty Images are models, and such images are being used for illustrative purposes only. Certain stock imagery © Getty Images.

ISBN: 978-1-6632-2034-9 (sc)
ISBN: 978-1-6632-2036-3 (hc)
ISBN: 978-1-6632-2035-6 (e)

Library of Congress Control Number: 2021912728

Printed in the United States of America.

iUniverse rev. date: 06/22/2021

Dedicated to those who perished on 9/11 and their surviving family members and loved ones.

We will never forget.

CONTENTS

Chapter One

CANCER

"Mr. Sanford, you have cancer."
The words echoed in my ears as the doctor pointed to the chest x-ray on the illuminator. It seemed like years, but only a few months earlier I'd had a routine chest x-ray at the annual fire department physical in Naples, Florida. Though I was the proverbial picture of health on the surface, an anomaly had been detected. They'd said it was probably a mistake, or possibly an error. But they called after the x-ray and asked me to come in for another look, just to be sure. The second visit confirmed my fears.

Three months passed from the discovery of cancer in July of 2007 until the treatment mapping in October. During that time, I told not a soul in my family or my inner circle. Our kids, all well into adulthood, were so worried about my wife, Maria, that I simply couldn't bring myself to add more stress or worry to any of their lives. We had been married for sixteen years, and Maria was in the fight of her life against her own illness: breast cancer.

For months, I flawlessly orchestrated and executed countless secret doctor appointments, biopsies, and follow-up appointments at the Naples Community Hospital. Every covert appointment went undetected by friends, family, and most of my coworkers.

One idle Sunday morning, Maria and I were about to leave for our favorite breakfast spot, the Cove Inn on Naples Bay. She was sitting in the kitchen with a straw hat on the table in front of her. She was thin, frail even, and without hair from the effects of her numerous cancer treatments. But this secret had been gnawing at my gut for long enough, and I'd finally decided to tell everyone. I had reached breaking point. I had to have treatment, and there was no hiding what was about to happen even if I wanted to.

I walked over to Maria and knelt beside her chair. My face felt hot, and I know I flushed bright red. I took her hand and said, "I have something really terrible to tell you.

I have lung cancer. They think that it's probably from New York, from 9/11."

This confession was one of the hardest things I've ever had to do. Tears poured out of us both; but, like the marvel she was, Maria became instantly focused, despite being blasted by this horrible news. Then again, what was she supposed to do?

I said to her, "I have not told anyone else, but it was discovered in July."

Always the voice of reason and always an incredibly positive person, Maria immediately said, "All right, Jerry. It is going to be OK. We are going to be OK." She had a way of saying things like she meant them—as if she could will them to be true.

Finishing my confession, I told her that I had already made arrangements to travel to Tampa and would be leaving soon. Maria asked, "What's up there?"

And I replied, "Moffitt. The cancer center."

Under different circumstances, I would have probably gone to Memorial Sloan Kettering, but New York City was simply too far to go for surgery. I knew traveling would not be possible for Maria, due to her failing health. In all honesty,

I could not have gone very far myself. My physical and emotional plate was full—overflowing, in fact.

I sort of recalled chatter, a rumor, that someone in the office had been treated locally—a battalion chief by the name of John Reilly. The world is very small, especially when it comes to Southwest Florida. Ironically, Reilly had attended the same high school on Staten Island as my oldest son, Glenn.

One day, when I saw Reilly walking down the hall at Station 45 in Naples, I asked if I could speak with him and pulled him into an empty office. After closing the door, I said, "I heard through the grapevine ... from some of the boys in the house ... can I ask you something confidentially? Did you have a cancer surgery?"

He answered the question with a question: "Why do you ask?"

I replied, "Well, between you, me, and this desk, I need surgery for cancer, and I can't make it to New York City."

Reilly interrupted me. "Hold on," he said. He fumbled with his phone, punched in some stuff, scribbled down a number on a scratch piece of paper, and said, "Call him. He's a thoracic surgeon up at Moffitt. He's the guy who is going to save your life, Jerry."

It turned out that Moffitt was the closest major specialized cancer treatment center. Although it was still a few hours away, it was the most logical choice for treatment.

Over the coming months, two surgeries were performed by Dr. Lary-with-one-R Robinson at Moffitt Cancer Center. My right lung was operated on in December, and nearly two months later to the day, my left lung was operated on. Now all that remains of my cancer is the set of "angel wing" removal scars on my back.

My post-surgery monitoring was completed in Bonita Springs under the care of Dr. Rubin at Florida Cancer Specialists. In 2012, Rubin discovered the cancer had returned, and he implemented the treatment. In total, there were fourteen chemotherapy treatments and thirty-five radiation treatments. I'm still sporting the souvenirs of radiation ink on my chest and each side of my rib cage. And I was one of the luckier cancer patients at Florida Cancer Specialists.

With mercy and flexibility from the department, I was able to continue working through it all. Eventually, the cancer beast was slain, and I walked away none the worse for wear. I still follow up annually for screenings, both with the World Trade Center Medical Monitoring Program in

New York City and with Dr. Rubin in Florida. Rubin calls me his "Miracle Man." I'm one of the few patients who has been fortunate enough to walk out of the fire, so to speak.

Sadly, Maria lost her battle with cancer in October of 2009, nearly two years to the day after I confessed my cancer secret to her. It was a long, grueling battle, and there is not a soul who put up a greater fight than she did. She was laid to rest near her first husband, Ted, the father of her children, at Naples Memorial Gardens. It is close to our home and to Vanderbilt Beach, where it is sunny and warm. It is exactly what she'd wished for.

Chapter Two

A FAILED RETIREMENT

Firefighters almost always have a second job, even a third. They have multiple streams of income, both out of necessity and sometimes due to lack of business acumen. In my early years, you name it, I did it. I painted with my brother-in-law's Uncle Benny. I was a furniture mover with Uncle Mickey. I was even a travel agent.

Travel became my second office. The travel agency is where I actually met Maria. Like me, she was recently divorced and working as a travel agent. We dated for years before we married in a simple ceremony in our apartment, officiated by a local judge.

Maria is also how I wound up in Naples. Her ex-husband, Ted, enjoyed the area and became a local restaurateur with their son, Paul. In the mid-1990s, a few years after Maria and I had gotten together, we started visiting Naples for vacations. Like most folks who visit Southwest Florida, after a few visits, we started thinking about putting down roots.

It's not exactly a difficult decision to abandon New York winters, the gray gloomy skies, and the concrete jungle of the city. In 2000, we rented a home in North Naples for about a year before taking the plunge and deciding to stay permanently. We eventually purchased a home and became official Florida retirees.

If you'd have told me forty years ago that I would be living in Southwest Florida, I wouldn't have believed it. I'd driven through the area a few times when it was all palmetto-lined one-lane roads. A portion of them were just dirt or crushed shells at that time. It was the true Old Florida, the good old days.

My first wife, Barbara, and I had taken our boys, Glenn and David, on many camping trips through the years. We drove through the area by way of Tamiami Trail on our way back from Key West. Interstate 75, also known as Alligator Alley, hadn't been constructed yet. We dragged our pop-up camper, complete with spare-tire cover that read "Sanford

& Sons," right through Naples. We even stayed at Oscar Scherer State Park, just south of Sarasota.

Like the typical retiree in Southwest Florida, about six months into living in paradise, I had golfed all the golf I could possibly golf and was around the house annoying my wife regularly. I was constantly underfoot and bumping into her. One day, she busted me strategically reorganizing the dirty dishwasher for her. I was told, in no uncertain terms, to find something to do with myself.

Of all things, I signed myself up for a Saturday afternoon CPR course that was advertised in the *Naples Daily News*. I would be out from under Maria's feet for one day, at least.

Emergency Medical Services Chief Diane Flagg was supervising the class in Naples. When the course was over, I walked up to her, introduced myself as a retiree from the FDNY, and asked her for a job. She probably thought I was nuts, but I handed her my card anyway. She said she already had a public information officer (PIO) and called him over.

His name was Jorge Aguilera, and he was a stocky guy with a smile always hidden under his mustache. We were introduced, and then Jorge said that he knew of another fire district that had a PIO who was going to be leaving the position and the area.

I was confused that there were multiple fire departments in such a small region. He further explained that Naples had more than one fire department. There were many fire districts in the area, each with its own staff. Coming from New York City, I found it mind-blowing that a location with this small a population had multiple departments or districts.

Unbeknownst to me, at some point Jorge gave my card to the chief at North Naples Fire Control and Rescue District. The following Monday, when I returned from golfing, I was met at the door by Maria, who said, "Hey, Grandpa, looks like you've gone and found yourself a job. Some chief named Jim Tobin called here today asking for you and wants you to come in."

She had apparently spoken to him on the phone for about an hour. Later that day, I called Tobin and made an appointment to be interviewed the very next day.

Complete with a freshly printed résumé and sporting my ultra-slick New York–style suit and red power tie, I headed into the chief's office. The interview consisted of me handing him my résumé, which he tossed on the edge of his desk and never even looked at again. We talked about the FDNY and fires, and we even listened to the Brooklyn scanner online for a few minutes. He listened to Brooklyn with the enthusiasm of a real buff.

After a while, he nonchalantly said, "See that white Crown Vic parked out there? That's your car." Just like that, I was hired as the PIO for North Naples Fire Control and Rescue District.

I had managed to fail at retirement in a whopping six months. Old habits die hard. I'd worked since I was eleven years old, beginning at La Tourette Golf Course on Staten Island. I should have known retirement wouldn't last. I officially went back to work in the fire service full time in May of 2000.

Chapter Three

NYPD TO FDNY

There is absolutely no doubt that my career in New York City blasted open the door in Naples. Thank goodness they didn't see how I crawled my way into the fire service industry the first time. My illustrious career as a firefighter, and I mean that sarcastically, actually began as a cop, where I worked in the seventh precinct on the Lower East Side.

Now, mind you, this was back in the 1960s, and you had to take a test to get hired. So I took the required tests to get on the hiring list for both the cops and the firefighters. I scored higher for the cops, and the police department called me first, so that's where I ended up. I knew getting in with the cops would also build some time toward a pension with the city, so naturally I took the job.

Unfortunately, this meant giving up my job on Wall Street and taking a tremendously painful pay cut. My first wife, Barbara, was less than thrilled with the economic downturn of our family finances. In 1965, the starting salary for an NYC police officer was a whopping $7,032—a figure forever burned into my brain. We ate a lot of hot dogs for a while, and trust me, Barbara made sure I heard about the pay cut every paycheck.

On the day I got sworn into the police department, a spastic bladder sent me to the men's room. I was so nervous, and I must have been white as a sheet. I'm standing at the urinal, and there's an old hair-bag detective standing next to me with a big cigar, puffing up a smoke storm.

The detective said in his finest New York accent, "Whassamatter, kid? Why you all white? You gettin' sworn in?"

I nervously nodded yes. I was a kid at the age of twenty-seven, which, at that time, was considered old to be launching a career in civil service. So there I was, married with a newborn baby and struggling to pay for a new house without a blade of grass in the yard. I was scared shitless by life before I even ended up in the police department, surrounded by this cloud of cheap cigar smoke. In fact, I think I was about to pass out.

The detective continued, "Don't worry about it, you're gonna love the job. What did you do before this?"

I replied, "I worked on Wall Street."

He retorted, "Don't worry about Wall Street. It's going down the tubes anyway." Then he said some words I didn't understand at the time, but they will stick with me for the rest of my days: "With the cops, the Eagle shits every two weeks no matter how bad the economy is." Then he zipped up his fly, blew a big puff of cigar smoke in my face, and walked away.

God bless all the hardworking men and women in blue … but within the first hour, I knew that being a cop was not for me. It just wasn't a fit for my personality. I hated writing a summons almost as much as I hated arresting people. I'd rather help people all day long than cause them a moment of strife.

Besides the typical duties of chasing bad guys, there were also not-so-glamorous overnight hours in freezing temperatures, staring at a fire box to make sure some jackass did not pull the alarm. Oh, and don't forget all the miserable hours of paperwork at the end of the shift. There was absolutely nothing glitzy or feel-good about the job, and I had to keep reminding myself that it was simply a miserable means of getting my foot in the door at the fire department.

I started out at the Seventh Precinct on the Lower East Side of Manhattan. One day, while I was chasing a criminal across rooftops, it occurred to me that I could get shot over a job I didn't even enjoy. That's when I quit running after the bad guys. I was about 140 pounds soaking wet and probably looked more like Barney Fife than Barney Miller.

Even if I had loved the job, there were plenty of other signs that law enforcement was not going to be a long-term career for me. Like the time I delivered someone to Bellevue Hospital and removed the bullets from my gun, as required while on the premises. It wasn't until I had completed my shift later that evening and emptied my pockets of loose bullets that I realized I had been on patrol the whole night without arming my weapon.

Not that bullets in my gun would have really made a difference anyway. When I was a rookie training at the range, my target often returned without a single bullet hole in it. One time, my sergeant came over, lifted my ear protection, and said, "Sanford, if you don't hit the fucking target, I'm going to take back your gun and issue you a spear."

4

Honestly, the NYPD doesn't know how lucky they were to lose me to the FDNY. By God's grace, I started working in fire in June of 1968. After I completed the training academy, when they were calling out assignments to the probies, I heard the training instructor shout, "Sanford, 23!" I had been assigned to Ladder 23.

My naivety ran away with my common sense, and I began scanning the map on the wall with my index finger, looking for the firehouse on Twenty-Third Street in Manhattan. After the laughter in the room subsided, I was swiftly corrected and informed that I was heading to Harlem. Ladder 23 is located at 139th and Amsterdam Avenue, even to this day.

The painful commute took me an hour and a half to two hours, each way, every day. I did that grind for nearly five years. There wasn't a single day that went by when I didn't wonder how many perfectly good firehouses I passed between my home on Staten Island and my job in Harlem.

In those days, if it was a total beater but the wheels still rolled, that's what I was driving. It was the "war years," and the mean streets of New York City were no place for a decent car, especially in Harlem between the late 1960s and the early 1970s. Jerry Motors, at your service! Every daily driver I owned required constant work to keep going, but that was back in the day when a regular guy could actually work on and repair a vehicle.

The balance of my ladder-truck career in the 1970s was at Ladder 131 in Red Hook, Brooklyn, where we were known as the Happy Hookers. It's pronounced Happy *Hookuhz* if you're from New York. While I loved my brothers at 23 Truck at Vinegar Hill in Harlem, I asked to be closer to home, as my first wife, Barbara, had some medical issues. At the time, I had two young boys, and I needed to shave off some of my commute time to spend with my family.

🚒

A few years later, I ended up in the 48 Battalion as an aide for Chief Don Ruland. This was around the time that Barbara and I divorced. The chief and I stayed together and then moved to the 21 Battalion on Staten Island, which eventually led to working at fire headquarters. Shortly after we transferred to headquarters, Don went on medical leave. His departure left me rattling around headquarters as an aide, working on special assignments and occasionally driving a fire chief around the city. Whatever they needed, I did it.

Working daily at fire headquarters presented the opportunity to be reunited with two old friends: Chief Bill Feehan, who was the chief of the department, and Charlie Rivera, who was the fire commissioner.

After some time had passed at headquarters—and unbeknownst to me—both Bill Feehan and Charlie Rivera orchestrated a scheme to get me into the press office. They both knew my work history and the time I had put in on the job. They knew that I knew the city like the back of my hand.

Frank Martinez, a lieutenant in the press office, stopped by one afternoon and told me that he was going to be leaving the position and there would be an opening in the press office. We talked, and he told me that I should really consider taking his place. I was leaving for vacation and would be gone for about a week, so he told me to think about it while I was away.

Honestly, it wasn't something I felt compelled to jump at. Nobody ever wanted to go to headquarters for work. It was the kiss of death for most firefighters. If you got put on light duty from an injury and you were told to go to headquarters, it was like getting sent to Alcatraz. I mean, who would want to sit at a desk inside when you can be riding on a screaming fire engine with the sights, sounds, and smells of New York City blasting you in the face?

Also, I knew two-times-nothing about the press, being a press secretary, or communications strategies. If ever there was a fish-out-of-water scenario, I was the living, breathing example of it.

My wife, Maria, encouraged me to try the job and reminded me that the worst that could possibly happen is that I ended up back in a firehouse. When I returned from vacation, I walked into Chief Feehan's office and told him about my conversation with Frank Martinez. Bill sort of bashfully hung his head low, like a little kid in trouble, and I could tell he was smirking and laughing. I finally said, "Chief, what the hell is going on?"

He motioned for me to close the door and, just as I did, he said, "Me and Charlie, we been talking, and we want you in the press office. You got, what, twenty years in now? You've been all over the city, and I know you. I have worked with you in the field. The fix is in, Sanford, and you're not gettin' it. You're in, just take it."

Charlie Rivera walked in, shook my hand, and said, "Come on, Jerry. You've worked your way up. You've been around. We're looking for somebody good, and you fit the bill. You got any suits?"

I nodded yes.

He replied, "Tomorrow, wear a suit. No more fire uniform for you."

And just like that, I was working in the press office of the fire commissioner of the largest fire department in the world. Me, a scrawny Irish kid born and raised on Staten Island, with no more than a high school education. Only in America can a person wind up with an opportunity like that.

Chapter Four

THE PRESS OFFICE

O n my first day working in the press office, I suited up and went to meet the staff, which consisted of the secretary, Pilar, and two light-duty firefighters. Soon I was leaning over to Pilar, looking for guidance. I whispered, "I don't know what the fuck I am doing here."

She always laughed at me and said, trilling her r's, "Oh, Jerry, you're such a funny guy."

Maybe she thought I was joking, but most of the time I really didn't know what I was doing. I was just winging it.

Early on at the press office, I found myself sitting at a conference table with Charlie Rivera, the fire commissioner;

a handful of chiefs; and most of the key players. Truthfully, I don't even remember what the meeting was about, but I do remember that it was a big deal. Charlie had grown frustrated with the direction of the meeting and the lackluster solutions he had been presented with. He looked over at me and said, "Jerry, what do you think we should do?"

I was just sitting there with a blank pad of paper in front of me, tapping my pen. All the chiefs turn and looked at me, and I didn't have a damn clue what to really do. I opened my mouth and out fell the words, "Well, Commissioner, I guess we know the questions that the reporters are going to ask, so why are we acting like we're afraid? We have all the answers, right? Let's just get it over with. How bad could it be?"

There was a moment of silence, and then the commissioner balled up a piece of paper and threw it at his assistant, Joe Dierks, and yelled, "So, Jerry's got to come in here and tell us what to do because none of you can?"

Dierks shot me a look like *Shut the hell up, Jerry.*

I really didn't have anything to lose, so I made the point, and a few minutes later I was setting up for the first press conference of my life. I stepped behind the podium and announced that the fire commissioner was on his way. Charlie came down, took the questions, and got it over with.

It went well, but I was floundering on the inside through the whole thing.

The job became smoother with time after I had learned the routine. There was a lot going on in New York City, and the millions of people living there definitely provided me with tons of practice. It wasn't long before I would walk into city hall early and take charge of an entire chaotic situation. There was always friendly animosity between cops and firefighters. The cops thought their shit didn't stink. Well, I was an ex-cop, and I thought the same.

I'd walk into the council chamber knowing the commissioner, Charlie Rivera, would be following me. I'd walk around the room and look at the name tags on the tables. They'd read *Inspector This* or *Inspector That*. Then I'd see the fire department nameplates, and it was like, *Why are we the ugly stepchild pushed way to the back in a corner?*

I'd say, "Screw this. This ain't happening." Then I'd pick up the nameplates and rearrange them in a manner more befitting to my fire department. I'd put the cops in the back, and I'd put the fire department up front.

The cops would arrive and come in all up in arms, thinking that they had somehow been demoted to the back. After a while, they figured out who I was and what I was about. I enjoyed the game of nameplate musical chairs; I would just stand there and grin. I'd send them a highball salute to acknowledge them when they recognized that they had just been played.

Then, when the fire commissioner came in, I'd make a big deal and be really loud about making sure he was summoned to his saved seat. The commissioner would walk toward me with these big, huge eyes, and you could almost read his mind: *Wha … what the hell am I doing in the front with the mayor?*

That was a classic Jerry job. That was the best part about being a former cop. I got balls being a cop. Bigger balls than I ever thought I'd have, in spite of the fact that I sucked on the gun range and hated arresting people.

My tenure in the press office sort of put me in charge, but I wasn't the official press secretary. After the next election, when the political winds changed direction, so did the ancillary players in the game.

One day, on my way out the door to grab lunch, I passed a dashing man wearing a suit in the lobby of fire headquarters. I thought he was Mayor Ed Koch's bodyguard. It turned out that he was actually Mayor Ed Koch's press secretary, Tom Kelly. Dinkins had been elected, so there was a changing of the guard. Kelly was landing in the FDNY press office, and we met in the lobby on his first day of work.

I said, "Hey, you're the guy who's on TV with Mayor Koch all the time."

He reached out his hand and said, "I'm Tom Kelly, and I've heard a lot about you, Jerry. Right now, all that I know is that fire engines are red, so you need to teach me all about this fire department; and I'm going to teach you how to be a reporter. It's going to be you and me."

That's exactly how the Tom and Jerry Show began, and boy, did we have some bromance. Kelly knew everyone, and we became nearly inseparable. We kicked ass all over the Big Apple, and we had a blast doing it. Think of a job that you loved and combine it with the fact that you were working with your best friend; that's what it was like for me working with Kelly. He taught me a lot, but most importantly, he taught me how to treat the press.

One of the early lessons was to never forget that reporters are people and they have a job to do. Even when they ask tough questions, just give them their story and be cooperative so that they can get on their way and get their job done. Then they'll leave you alone.

Honestly, I'm not exactly sure if I learned this before or after I gave a smart-ass response to a reporter. She had called and asked a ridiculously stupid question about an explosive fire outside of Grand Central Station during a terrible snowstorm. At some point of frustration with the conversation, I sarcastically barked that there were manhole covers flying around like pizzas and then hung up the phone. Well, "manhole covers were flying everywhere" ended up in the *New York Times* the next morning, with my name on the quote. Way to go, Sanford!

Lessons of humility and patience were learned quickly. All my friends were so kind as to cut the article out of the paper and share it with me.

Kelly was a badass who knew his job and oozed confidence. We called city hall "the hall." We'd walk into the hall and cruise right past the metal detectors without anyone even blinking an eye. Kelly was absolutely fearless, and he was a maestro at orchestrating events and influencing the attitude of the crowd. When we started working together, I was consistently caught off guard when an event turned on a dime and went precisely the way he intended it to.

One day, we were graduating a class of probies out at the rock, which was the training center. At the time, the fire union was really having a beef with Mayor Dinkins. Dinkins was supposed to be the keynote speaker at the graduation ceremony, and it was not expected to go very well. I remember telling Kelly that the guys were going to go nuts when the mayor walked out there—that they were going to boo the shit out of him.

Kelly waved me off and said, "Don't worry about it. I got it."

So, everyone was assembling in the auditorium, and I was looking around, but I couldn't find Kelly anywhere. I continued going through my whole public relations checklist and routine. I had everything ready. The program lineup was in order for the ceremony to begin.

In walked Mayor Dinkins. He sat up onstage with the fire commissioner. Captain Brian Dixon was the emcee. He introduced the panel and then said, "And now, it is my distinct pleasure to introduce to you the mayor of New York City, Mayor David Dinkins."

Inside my head, I was thinking, *Oh, shit*, and mentally bracing for the blowback of angry firefighters. And then I heard whistles—not whistling like a song, but whistling like we're at a Rolling Stones concert cheering for an encore. It wasn't just one whistler, either. There was whistling and clapping from the balcony in several strategic locations.

Peer pressure is an amazing thing. The whole audience burst into applause and whistled, following along with the artfully planted whistlers, one of whom I realized was Tom Kelly. I saw him with his index fingers dug into the corners of his mouth, leading the whistle charge from the left balcony. He looked down at me as I was looking up at him, laughing my ass off as I watched him turn what should have been a room full of booing into cheers and applause.

Eventually, when Rudy Giuliani was elected, Kelly left the press office. He moved on to the corrections office as their spokesperson and eventually became the deputy commissioner for public information with the cops. Upon his departure, I was promoted to press secretary. Though the Tom and Jerry Show had come to an end, the lessons learned were a lifelong gift.

Chapter Five

THE HELMET

Some people call it six degrees of separation, the thin red thread of destiny, or just fate—but sometimes, we're all in the right place at the right time, or even the wrong place at the right time. Two of the consistent threads running through my life have been the fire department and New York City. In Southwest Florida, I had become the guy from New York City, and that commonality was applied to multiple situations. If it involved the Big Apple, my phone rang.

Actually, my phone rang all the time, for just about any sort of problem. Maria used to joke, "Why wouldn't they call you for [insert ridiculous problem]? Just dial 1-800-Call-Jerry."

There was a time in about 2016 when someone called to have me move the planes from one side of the Naples Municipal Airport to the other to make room for an event. Keep in mind, I am not a pilot. I had nothing to do with the airport, nor did I know anyone *at* the airport. Long story short, I got the planes moved, but why someone would call me for that makes just about as much sense as any of the other requests I received.

When I started my second fire career in Naples, it wasn't long before Chief Tobin called me to tell me about an antique leather fire helmet. Apparently, a man by the name of George Kunze Jr. had walked into the North Naples Fire Department and donated it. The helmet had belonged to Kunze's father. It wound up hung on a wall in Station 44, which is in Pelican Bay in Naples.

I was probably only five or six weeks into my new job when I drove over to Station 44 with Chief Tobin to see the helmet. It was an old black leather fire helmet from about 1912 to 1914. I instantly knew that it was from New York City. It had the numbers 4-2 in red on the front, so I knew it was from the South Bronx. I also knew that particular firehouse because my former boss, Commissioner Tom Von Essen, worked in Ladder 42.

Talk about a small world. Here I was standing in Naples with a helmet from Von Essen's old firehouse. I exclaimed, "Wow, that's quite a helmet."

Tobin replied, "Do you think they'd want it back?"

Of course, I was sure that they would, and I told Tobin the same.

We drove back to our fire station, and I called fire headquarters and got Tommy on the phone. I let him know that I had gotten another job. He immediately started abusing me the way firefighters have a special way of doing: "Who would hire you? We just got rid of you. What a disaster of a mistake they've made."

I soaked up all the friendly ribbing; we in the brotherhood gave each other playful jabs like that regularly. Tommy and I caught up a little, and I filled him in on where I was, how I got hired by another fire department, and that I had come into possession of an old fire helmet from his company. I said, "We'd like to bring it back sometime and present it to the company."

He replied, "Sure, but why don't you wait to bring it back. Right now, the firehouse is going through a huge renovation, and it won't be complete until summer 2001."

From time to time, I'd follow up on the progress of Ladder 42 and speak to Frank Gribbon. Frank had taken my place when I retired, and he was my contact for finding out when the renovation of 42 was going to wrap up. It was June 2001 when I spoke to Frank again, and he told me they had finally set a date for the firehouse rededication ceremony: September 10.

Of course, September 10, 2001, meant nothing to me or anyone else at that time. It was merely another date on the calendar.

Chapter Six

SEPTEMBER 10

O n September 8, George Kunze Jr., Chief Tobin, Battalion Chief Wayne Jones, and I made our way to New York City. We were only going to be in town for a couple of days, so we stayed at a hotel in Long Island City, fairly close to the Bronx. We took a whirlwind tour of New York City, mostly by way of my old firehouses. The Florida boys wanted to see where I had worked, so we stopped in at Ladder 23 in Harlem, Ladder 131 in Brooklyn, the communications center, and a few other places.

It was a different world, and it made Naples look like a sleepy village. The boys ate it up. There was a ton to see and do, but we didn't do any tourist sightseeing, such as visiting the Statue of Liberty or the World Trade Center.

On the morning of September 10, we arrived at Ladder 42 in the South Bronx to participate in the ceremony by presenting the helmet to the fire captain. The stage was set for the ceremony, including an altar for Father Mychal Judge. He was a Brooklyn native and one of the fire department's Catholic chaplains. Nobody could have imagined that it was the last mass he would ever say. He was one of the first members of the department to be killed the next day. There is an iconic photo of firefighters carrying his lifeless body from the scene of the World Trade Center towers.

The ceremony went off without a hitch. It was a great time, and I was reunited with the fire staff I had worked with as well as Mayor Rudolph Giuliani, whom I had also previously worked with. Father Judge said mass, and it was followed by the ribbon-cutting ceremony and the presentation of the helmet back to the captain of Ladder 42.

After the ceremony, many of us went to a nearby Dominican social club, where we had cold cut sandwiches and drinks and socialized with all the guys, many of whom were killed the next day. I sat with chief of the department, Pete Ganci, and ribbed him about coming to Florida and experiencing the good life. I chided him to come down and golf with me, and I handed him my business card from North Naples Fire.

The party wrapped up shortly thereafter, and we all said our goodbyes. Father Judge blessed me and kissed me goodbye, and then the "helmet party" from Naples drove to LaGuardia Airport and turned in the rental car. We checked in with the airline, made our way to the terminal gate, and were all set to fly back to Fort Myers, Florida.

Chapter Seven

SEPTEMBER 11

Most people remember exactly where they were on September 11, but what many of them don't remember is how bad the weather was in New York City on September 10. Sometime around the dinner hour, it started to rain. It rained so hard that our flight was eventually delayed. The rain continued, and then our flight was finally canceled.

Shortly after, all the departing flights were canceled. In fact, flights were canceled at all three airports in the New York City area. The airport was in complete chaos, but we were able to get our flights rebooked for the next morning,

September 11. We were spending another night in New York.

Maria's daughter, Jean, lived in Westchester County, so we called her for room and board. She sent her husband, Michael, to pick us up. We were able to grab a quick bite to eat and spent the night at their place. We were up at four in the morning and driven back to the airport, where we caught our flight to Florida, with a change of planes in Pittsburgh. It didn't occur to me until years later that we could have been on a hijacked plane.

Ironically, as we flew out of LaGuardia Airport, we traveled perpendicular to Manhattan Island right down the East River, heading south. Looking out the window, I showed George and Wayne the skyline and pointed out the United Nations Building, the Chrysler Building, the Empire State Building, the Statue of Liberty, the World Trade Center, and Staten Island, home of the world's largest garbage dump and the place I called home for most of my life.

We arrived in Pittsburgh to change planes, and as we were about to get onto our connecting flight, Wayne decided to hit the head before boarding. It was about a quarter before nine in the morning. I was waiting in the corridor for Wayne when I heard him scream my name and saw him frantically waving. "Jerry, come down here! Hurry up!" he yelled.

He was pointing to a television, and that was the first sight I had of what was unfolding. One of the Twin Towers was on fire. We watched with the rest of the world and tried to grasp how a plane had accidentally flown into one of the buildings. We still had a flight to complete, so we made our way down the terminal and boarded our plane. I must have had a look of shock on my face, because the captain of the plane actually stopped me and asked if I was OK. I said something to the effect that a plane had just flown into the World Trade Center.

With that, the pilot ended up getting off the plane, and I took my seat. Not long after I was situated, the captain came back on board and explained that there had been some sort of air mishap in New York City. He backed the plane out, and we taxied a couple hundred yards and stopped. Then a voice came on the intercom and said that the FAA had grounded all flights.

As passengers, we really didn't know what had happened. We just knew our plane was being turned around, and we were getting off with hundreds of passengers from other planes that were also being turned around. The passengers from our flight spilled out into the terminal, directly into an airport that was in total pandemonium. It was like we had stepped into an alternate universe.

We split up and each got on line with a car rental agency to see if we could get a vehicle and get out of the airport. With a car secured, our first stop was to buy a map and get a charger for my cell phone, as I had packed my charger in my suitcase. This was before everyone had a phone with map apps. We had the radio on in the car, and we hung on every word.

We learned that a second plane had hit the South Tower. The Pentagon had also been hit, and a plane had gone down in Shanksville, Pennsylvania. America was under attack! The boys wouldn't let me drive because I was in total shock. I knew from my career in the fire service exactly what was going on in New York City. The first responders, my brothers, were running into those buildings while everyone else was running out. I knew they were climbing those stairs. I was torn and sick to my stomach. I just wanted to be on-site, because I knew it was bad—unbelievably bad, the worst the city had ever seen. I had responded to the bombing of the World Trade Center in 1993, but this—this terrorism—was uncharted territory.

Listening to radio reports, we learned that the towers had collapsed. I was in absolute disbelief, as I had driven past them every day while they were being built in the 1960s going to Ladder 23 in Harlem. To me, it was impossible. I was literally screaming at the radio, yelling that they were full of shit, because I just couldn't believe it had happened.

We pulled into a rest area, and there was a TV on with the news. That was the first time I saw the cloud with the buildings gone. Everyone was standing in the restaurant staring at the television in utter disbelief.

From the rest area, I called fire headquarters in Brooklyn. One of the secretaries, Lisa, answered the phone and was hysterical. I could barely understand her. Everyone in headquarters was crying inconsolably and passing the phone around. One of them said, "They're all gone, Jerry! All of them! Gone! They're all dead!" I had just been with them the day before, and they were gone? I couldn't even begin to process what was happening.

🜂

We drove all night. Our first stop was the Fort Myers Airport (RSW) because we needed to pick up our car and our luggage. Remember: we were originally flying out on the tenth, and our bags were on that plane. We'd ended up spending an extra day in New York and then a day driving back to Florida, with only the clothes on our back.

The road into RSW was blocked by the Florida Highway Patrol. We "tinned" them, which means we flashed our badges, and told them what was going on. We said we were going to try to get our bags and cars from the parking lot.

Going into an airport that is completely shut down the way RSW was is an eerie feeling and hard to comprehend. The four of us walked in, and there wasn't a soul inside—not a person in the airport. We yelled, "Hello! Hello! Is anyone here?" Finally, someone responded, but they were terrified of us because everyone was afraid of more terror attacks. We showed our IDs and badges, and they explained that they had no idea where our bags were, but any baggage would be delivered when the airport resumed operation.

The attack was on Tuesday morning, the same day we flew out. We were finally home Wednesday evening. On Thursday, I went to the North Naples fire station, and everyone wanted to know what was going on. Tobin walked in, and I looked at him and said, "Look, Chief, I'm going back to New York City. I don't care if I lose my job. I just gotta go back."

Tobin replied, "Go, Jerry. This job will be waiting for you to get back."

By coincidence, Maria and I had purchased airline tickets, months earlier, to fly to Philadelphia on the Saturday following 9/11. We were going to attend the christening of our grandson, Jack Ryan Kennedy. By that time, the FAA had allowed flights to resume. We got on a plane with fewer than ten other people who were brave enough to board. Everyone was terrified to fly.

We attended the christening on Sunday, and after dinner, I called headquarters and spoke to Von Essen, letting him know I was in Philadelphia and that I wanted to come back and help.

He said, "Jerry, whenever you can, please come back. We need all the help we can get."

On Monday morning, I borrowed a car and drove from Philadelphia to New York City. On the way, I stopped and met my oldest son, Glenn, at a rest stop on the Garden State Parkway. I just wanted to see him, hug him, and say goodbye because it was the craziest time. I just didn't know what could happen next.

By the end of the day, I was at fire headquarters in Brooklyn. A work colleague and dear friend, Paul Iannizzotto, drove me to the 9/11 site. Six days after the attack, I was standing on the pile, looking down at firefighters who were climbing all over, searching for people and remains. The mountain of scorched rubble was so huge that the men almost looked like ants. The acrid trail of smoke drifted across the East River to Brooklyn and Queens.

Downtown Manhattan looked like a Third World, war-torn nation. Government officials claimed that the air was safe. Years later, those working on the pile and many in the general vicinity would fall victim to cancers and other illnesses caused by 9/11.

We remained at the site for a few hours, and then Paulie drove me back to headquarters. That night, I slept in my old office on the couch. The next morning, I took my orders to be part of Mayor Giuliani's press team, once again representing the largest and greatest fire department in the world: the FDNY.

This page is intentionally left blank in remembrance of the 343 firefighters who lost their lives on September 11, 2001.

Chapter Eight

BACK ON THE JOB

The weeks that followed were grim. Our days were filled with funerals: planning funerals, attending funerals, burying friends and brothers, sometimes burying them twice. Keep in mind that 343 men in one fire department were gone in an instant. Slowly read that number again … 343. Besides the emotional toll of loss and despair, the sheer number of people missing was an enormous void to fill.

The department was in absolute chaos from every angle. From the personnel standpoint, firefighters were being promoted like crazy because so many battalion chiefs, captains, and lieutenants had died in the collapse. Probies were put to work immediately, and volunteers came from all over the country to help with the rescue and recovery effort. Daily there was a report of someone's body, or a part of the body, being found.

Weeks after my arrival, I was working at the FDNY press office, trying to organize the chaos. It was really late, like nine or ten at night, and I heard some movement, some men talking. Someone yelled, "Is Jerry here?"

So I got up and yelled, "Here!"

It was a couple of fire marshals I knew from back in the day. We exchanged pleasantries, given the nature of the circumstances that were reuniting us. They said that Pete Ganci's body had been recovered, and one of them stretched out his arm and handed me my business card back.

Pete was the highest-ranking uniformed officer on the ground that day. He was last seen entering the North Tower. Later, his radio was recovered from beneath the rubble of the fallen towers. Pete's body was recovered with my business card in his pocket. It was a moment of shock and loss that can only be experienced, not described by words.

🜚

Initially, I lived in my office, and then on the hospital ship *USNS Hope*. Finally, I tracked down Frank "Cookie" McCarton, who had once worked for me but had been transferred to Giuliani's office. I asked him to get me a decent place to sleep, where someone's ass wasn't in the bunk above my head.

He left and returned about an hour later, saying, "You're staying at the Waldorf."

A few hours after that, a few New York State Troopers show up asking for Commissioner Sanford. They explained that they had been assigned to drive the commissioner anywhere he needed to go and that they were to drop him off at the Waldorf. Of course, I didn't correct them about me not being a commissioner … at least not right away. I did, however, ask them to cut off the lights and sirens, and to take me to Macy's for underwear before they dropped me at the hotel.

It was quite an experience going from a christening to New York City, then to my office, then to the ship, and then to the hotel. In that short time, I had amassed quite a collection of items, including fire gear and plastic bags full of various items and toiletries, plus my new underwear from Macy's department store. It was quite an interesting look, bordering on hobo; and I was being dropped off at one of the most famous hotels in the world.

All the doors to the hotel were closed, except for one that had a guard stationed by a metal detector. I was verified as a guest and cleared. As I entered, I looked up the beautiful stairs. That's where I had imagined all the famous celebrities and dignitaries ascending. Naturally, I would not make it up the stairs without dropping my classy plastic bags and watching my new underwear slide back to the entry in the slowest, most dramatic fashion. The universe and gravity had stepped in to remind me that I was just a temporarily displaced firefighter from Staten Island.

Chapter Nine

JAY JONAS

Josephine Harris worked at the Port Authority in the North Tower. She was a grandmother with a variety of health issues. One was a leg injury from an accident that had occurred before she worked in the tower.

On the day of the attack, there was pandemonium everywhere, and the tower next door was on fire. The North Tower had already been hit by a plane just above where Josephine was located. She had grabbed her pocketbook and started the trek down fifty-some flights of stairs.

About that same time, Ladder 6, with Captain Jay Jonas and a handful of firefighters, arrived at the scene and was directed to go up the tower. As they were going up, they started fanning out, floor by floor, looking for people to evacuate from the structure. They eventually crossed paths with Josephine somewhere around the twentieth floor.

They helped her down the stairs, but at around the fourth floor, her legs gave out. Josephine was exhausted and ordered Jonas to leave her. He refused and told her that they were all getting out of there—but as they started down the stairs, the tower started coming down on top of them. They were several stories above street level, with hundreds of tons of materials above and around them.

The tower collapsed, but when the initial collapse was over, they were alive, still in what remained of the stairwell. They were all spared by way of a miracle and eventually rescued from the rubble. It was called the Miracle of Stairwell B, and it was all over the news.

Things like this certainly don't happen every day. It's also not every day that the president of the United States of America, the leader of the free world, wants to recognize one of our firefighters for his heroism. That's exactly what happened next. The White House requested that Jay Jonas travel to Washington, DC, to be recognized for his leadership and bravery by President George W. Bush.

Ordinarily, this wouldn't have been too dramatic an event, except nobody really knew where Jay was. The city was still in complete upheaval, and the department had lost hundreds of men and women. It was all-hands-on-deck in the department.

It turned out that Jay was on duty in one of the battalions. He had been promoted to battalion chief as the department scrambled to fill vacant positions. When I found Jay, I told him that I had orders from the commissioner to relieve him of duty. Then I asked him where his dress uniform was. It was my job to make sure he had a dress uniform and was on that plane to DC to be recognized by the president.

Unfortunately, Jay's uniform was somewhere in upstate New York at a dry-cleaning shop. So I started peppering Jay with questions: "What size jacket do you wear? What's your waist size and length of pants?" I called around to the other battalions, trying to find clothes for a big guy. Then I sent people out all over to find and pick up each item of clothing.

I eventually pieced together a complete dress uniform for this presidential event. It was frantic, but we did it. We got him on the plane at LaGuardia, and then I immediately went back to work. There was always another crisis or issue to resolve.

I wanted to see the presidential address and to see if Jay made it to prime time. But as I drove away from work and over the Brooklyn Bridge that night, around eight thirty, everything south of Canal Street in Manhattan was pitch dark. There was no electricity anywhere. Imagine even ambient light from the smallest devices missing. It was apocalyptic. Not even doorbells or small lights in stores were working. Emergency lights had run out of juice days ago.

It was a dark like most people never experience. The streetlights were out. There were no working traffic signals, and people with flashlights were walking on the sidewalks. Plus, there were National Guard and police officers stationed as a presence everywhere, with their Jeeps parked in the street blocking restricted areas.

I was driving a department car as fast as I could in that environment, looking for someplace, any place, that might be open. I wanted to make sure I got to see the presidential address and, of course, see Jay Jonas recognized. I don't remember exactly where I was—I was probably near the Meatpacking District in the West Village—when I came across a rough-looking biker bar. The lights were on, so I parked the car and went in.

This joint was packed, because it was one of the few places in the area with electricity. There was shit-kicking music at full blast. Let's just say that these were not my people. I was wearing my red fire department jacket with *FDNY Press* across the back in reflective letters. I elbowed my way through the crowd and got to the back of the bar.

There were a half-dozen televisions on with various shows: cartoons, news, sports. I told the bartender that I was with the New York City Fire Department, and in a few minutes, the president was going to be on. I wanted every TV turned on to the presidential address.

He looked at me like a typical New Yorker would, like "Who the fuck are you?" and so I turned and pointed to my back, showing the FDNY lettering. This guy turned and walked over to the manager, still polishing a glass, and then pointed at me. The boss came over and said, "What's the problem?" I told him who I was and that I needed the TVs all turned to a major network for the presidential address at nine o'clock.

At one minute before nine, the boss took out the remote control and started flipping TVs to one of the major networks. The logo of POTUS was on the television screen, and then the president was on screen. The rowdy crowd fell quiet, and then everyone in the bar started chanting, "USA, USA, USA." It was like a scene from a movie.

I was now standing near the door of this crazy place, reduced to tears and watching this biker crowd go wild. The president addressed the nation and recounted the story of the Miracle in the Stairwell, then he recognized Jay Jonas in the gallery. Jay stood and acknowledged the president. What a moment! He looked great in the dress uniform. All the hours of scrambling for clothes in the midst of the work-related chaos had paid off, and our boy was in Washington, doing the FDNY proud.

A few weeks later, I ran into Jay at a funeral. We exchanged pleasantries, and I said something like, "So how was that trip to Washington?"

He replied, "It was great, Jerry. But we got lucky that they didn't pan down to my feet because I had sneakers on." I had clearly forgotten to scrounge him a pair of dress shoes to go with the uniform. He was well-dressed and wearing sneakers when he met the President of the United States.

Chapter Ten

TIME MARCHES ON

B eing involved with September 11 is like being a member of an exclusive club built around sorrow and loss. Decades later, I often wonder what ever became of some of the people from the FDNY and 9/11. I did stay in touch with a few people, but many of those relationships faded with time. Maybe it's because we are a reminder to each other of such a dark, sad time in our nation's history.

Some of us held on for a few years and then lost contact. Both Jay Jonas and Josephine Harris came to Naples, Florida, to speak at a September 11 ceremony that I organized in 2007. They shared their harrowing stories as the keynote speakers and left the audience slack-jawed, with tear-stained cheeks. After that event, we drifted apart. I was told that Jay continued working at the FDNY and that Josephine passed away in 2011.

Tom Von Essen, the fire commissioner, eventually retired from the FDNY. As the years passed, we fell out of touch. In 2017, I was watching Hurricane Maria coverage on the news from my home in Florida and, lo and behold, Von Essen popped up on the screen! I started screaming to my lady, Chris, "Honey, come look! Tom Von Essen is on the news!" Little did I know that in 2017, Von Essen had been appointed as a FEMA administrator for New York City by President Donald Trump.

I'm not sure where Kelly ended up after he was the deputy commissioner for public information with the cops. We were in two entirely different work orbits, and we drifted apart. We each retired and moved from the New York City area, which also created a physical gap. You're not exactly going to accidentally bump into someone when they're living in Colorado and you're living in Florida.

As luck would have it, in 2021, I called Tom Fitzpatrick, a retired lieutenant from the FDNY, to wish him happy birthday, and he said, "You're never gonna believe who I just spoke to ... Tom Kelly!"

Fitzpatrick filled me in on some of the cursory updates of what Kelly had been up to, and then he texted me Kelly's number. I dialed him up right away. We played a little phone tag but finally connected. We did our best to quickly fill in the nearly twenty-year gap since the Tom and Jerry Show. We agreed that too much time had gone by and that we would not let it happen again. Then we immediately connected on Facebook to make sure we'd not lose touch.

Sadly, my dear friend and mentor Bill Feehan was one of the 343 who lost their lives on September 11. He was a living legend who had held every rank within the FDNY. I knew so many of the people who perished that day and proudly display a poster of the lost firefighters, including Bill, on a wall in my home office.

From time to time, I will run into an FDNY retiree in Southwest Florida. Firefighters are not bashful about the job, most especially FDNY firefighters. They are usually wearing the logo on a hat, shirt, or bumper sticker bearing the Maltese cross. There's always warm conversation, in a thick New York accent, served with a helping of firehouse camaraderie.

It's called the brotherhood for a reason. We really are family. No matter where you are in the country, or even the world, you can walk into a firehouse and ask for help, use the bathroom, or just give them a hard time, especially the enginemen.

The one thing we really don't talk much about is 9/11 or the cancer we got from it. Nobody wants to hear a whole bunch of busted-up old firefighters sitting around comparing their medical procedures and cancers. I certainly don't want to relive the play-by-play of my rounds with cancer, anyway. Plus, I'm the one who got away, so I don't feel compelled to go back and rehash it.

Chapter Eleven

THE PEOPLE-
HELPING BUSINESS

T he path away from New York after 9/11 was uneventful. I slipped out of the city just as easily as I slipped in. Several weeks into my volunteer duty with the FDNY, overwhelming exhaustion and heartbreak was telling me that it was time to return to my new home in Naples. The weeks in New York had been painful and soul-draining. It's impossible to unsee the things that I saw or to forget about what happened in New York City.

I returned to my normal life and my normal job, but I no longer felt like normal Jerry. I resumed my work and my regular life in the best way I knew, and that was by helping people. I've been in the people-helping business all my life, so I jumped back in feetfirst.

My duties in Florida as the public information officer (PIO) for North Naples Fire introduced me to a myriad of possibilities—ways to help people both as individuals and as charitable organizations. One of my satisfying achievements was running and growing the Community Emergency Response Team (CERT) in North Naples. The program trains and prepares civilians for response prior to, during, and after a disaster, specifically the natural disaster of hurricanes in our area.

Through my involvement with CERT came another program called Serving Our Seniors (SOS), through which we organized and trained CERT members to shop and deliver groceries for those who were no longer able to shop for themselves but continued to live in their homes.

Another group was formed almost by accident. One of my first responses was to a brushfire in North Naples, and as PIO, I gave an interview on the evening news. It hadn't occurred to me that there would be all sorts of retired firefighters from the FDNY living in Southwest Florida, or that people I knew would actually be watching that broadcast. But my phone started ringing off the hook, and the reunions started happening. The boys couldn't believe

I was here, working again with the media, and that my weathered face was on their TV.

From there, it was almost a natural progression to form Gulf Coast Retired Firefighters to give the boys a way to meet and stay in touch. The organization is active to this day. There is nothing like the brotherhood, and many of these men not only fought fires with me but also helped with the next project I was involved in, funding the Freedom Memorial of Collier County.

A few years had passed after 9/11 when I was contacted by a Collier County commissioner, Fred Coyle, who asked if I was "the New York guy." He explained that there was an idea being floated to build a Freedom Memorial in Naples to honor the victims of 9/11, first responders, and the military. Commissioner Coyle, a retired colonel in the US Army, invited me to help form a task force to get the project off the ground, help select the design, and get it funded.

On paper, it seemed a doable task, but the reality was that it took well over a decade, countless penny-ante fundraisers, and a miracle to get the millions of dollars collected. Most of this project took place after the housing crisis of the early 2000s and the following recession, so it was painfully slow and difficult.

There was a public call put out for potential designs for the memorial, and a gentleman who was having a home built in Naples saw the request on the Collier County government website. His was one of just under forty design submissions. The submissions were eventually narrowed to three candidates, and the commissioners selected one at a Collier County Commissioners meeting.

At that final meeting, seated down the row from me, a man started weeping when the winner was announced. It was the designer and artist, Gerald Ladue. His vision of freedom and what it means to be an American is now a lasting legacy in Naples, Florida. Behind the granite memorial stand two rusted beams of steel from the World Trade Center.

Besides the lives I've saved on the job and my own personal sobriety of more than forty years, it is one of my greatest achievements. Every time I drive past it on Golden Gate Parkway, I salute it and say, "I'll never forget you, brothers."

The Freedom Memorial stands at Fred C. Coyle Freedom Park, located at 1515 Golden Gate Parkway, Naples, Florida. When you visit, say a prayer for my 343 brothers and sisters and the others who were lost that day. Never forget!

THE FREEDOM MEMORIAL IN NAPLES, FLORIDA.

EPILOGUE

Jerry Sanford currently resides in Naples, Florida, with his significant other, Chris Griffith, and their dog, Dillon. Jerry wishes to extend his gratitude to Chris for recording the stories and molding this book into its present format to share with the world.

North Naples Fire Control and Rescue District, where Jerry worked for seventeen years, merged with Big Corkscrew Island Fire District and became North Collier Fire Control and Rescue District. Jerry is now retired from North Collier Fire Control and Rescue District but occasionally performs master of ceremony duties for the fire district and graduations of new students from North Collier Fire School. A few years after Jerry's retirement, Chief Eloy Ricardo recognized and honored him for his dedication to the fire service by naming the training facility at Station 45 Sanford Hall. Jerry is profoundly grateful for the years spent at North Collier Fire Control and the great friends he made along the way.

Jerry currently spends much of his free time volunteering,

supporting, and chairing several charitable organizations in the Southwest Florida area, including Homer's Annex—Gulf Coast Veterans and Friends, Wounded Warriors of Collier County, Home Base, and the Bonita Springs Assistance Office.

Links to the charitable organizations mentioned in this book include the following:

- www.freedommemorialfoundationofnaples.org
- www.gulfcoastretiredfirefighters.com
- www.gulfcoastvf.org
- www.woundedwarriorsofcolliercounty.com
- www.homebase.org
- www.bonitaassistance.org
- www.wreathsacrossamerica.org

Students and Teachers

If you are a teacher or an administrator of education and would like to receive a complimentary copy of *It Started with a Helmet* for the classroom, visit the website and submit a request through the contact page at www.ItStartedWithAHelmet.com. Donations to help provide books to students are graciously accepted via the Freedom Memorial Foundation of Naples. Donated funds will assist with publication, clerical, and postage expenses. Visit the donate page at www.ItStartedWithAHelmet.com.

Never Forget!